Can Drivers Really Teach Themselves?

A Practitioner's Guide to
Using Learner Centred and
Coaching Approaches in
Driver Education

March 2011

Ian Edwards
MSc. Dip ASM., DSA ADI

Published by eDriving Solutions

Copyright © eDriving Solutions Ltd 2011

ISBN 978-0-9569711

Foreword

This is an invaluable guide for all professionals in the Driver Education and Training Industry. Ian is a highly qualified practitioner who has written this guide in a readable and concise fashion. His experience as an approved driving instructor shines from every page of the book, entitling him to offer practical advice on learner centred coaching to others. Our careers have intertwined over the last ten years and I have always found Ian to be dedicated to improving road safety with driver education and training.

I would particularly recommend the GROW plan as an essential tool to use for self-improvement and also as a positive approach to enabling learner drivers to evaluate their own driving skills.

I am certain this guide will become essential reading for all those involved in the profession.

Gillian Roberts
Senior Road Safety Officer, Dip.ASM
St Helens Council

The Author - Ian Edwards

Ian is one of the leading road safety practitioners in the UK. As well as being a qualified driving instructor since 1988 he holds a Master of Science Degree in Social Research and Evaluation and a Diploma in Traffic Accident and Safety Management.

As the only UK driving instructor on the Hermes Project, an EU funded project looking at the development of coaching skills for driving instructors, Ian has a unique view of coaching and learner centred approaches to Driver Education. Ian speaks widely on coaching and has lectured on the University of East London's Coaching for Driver Development course.

Ian's interests relating to driver education include:

> The role of self-evaluation in driver education
> Implementing the Goals for Driver Education
> e-learning
> Coaching skills
> Using social research methods to evaluate road safety interventions

Upon qualifying as a driving instructor Ian worked in a local instructor partnership until 1994, leaving to open and operate his own company specialising in instructor training. In 2000 Ian joined Doncaster's Road Safety Unit where he developed a number of schemes for young people, including a wheel chair user's course.

In 2001 he moved to Kirklees Metropolitan Council to manage the delivery of the National Driver Improvement Scheme across South and West Yorkshire. During this period Ian developed and evaluated the Kirklees Enhanced version of the DSA's Pass Plus course the outcomes of which won a Prince Michael of Kent Award and led to the Department of Transport commissioning research into the use of driver workshops in driver education. He was also heavily involved in the development of a driver training strategy for Kirklees which won an Institute of Civil Engineers Award (Yorkshire and Humberside) in 2005 for innovation. Over this period Ian served for 3 years as a member of the management group for the

Association of National Driver Improvement Scheme Providers.

In 2006 Ian left Kirklees M.C. to join a national driver training company as their Director of Education and in this role Ian oversaw the design and development of all elements of the curriculum, including 11 e-learning modules, an instructor training programme and an e-based learning management system. In 2008 Ian become a Transport Consultant and started the development of eDriving Solutions with Dave Parkin and Neil Beeson.

Ian is married to Julie and has four sons: Alex (17), Jake (14) Ashley (9) and Patrick (7). He has drawn heavily on the wonderful experiences he shares with his family in the development of his work.

Contents

Acknowledgements

So many people have helped to develop this book it is impossible to mention them all. My family, Julie and the boys deserve special thanks for creating the time for me to undertake this work, as does Moyra, my sister, for spending countless hours proof reading and correcting text. As to all the friends who have commented, discussed and put up with my constant talking on this subject you have made this much better than I could have done alone - *thank you.*

1. Using this book

Please take a moment to read this section before you start to read the rest of this book.

This book is aimed at driving instructors and road safety professionals across the world with an interest in improving and developing the way that driver education is delivered and learnt. It focuses on how to use learner centred and coaching techniques in driver education rather than what to teach. I have presumed in writing this book that you, the reader, already have a good level of knowledge – pitching the book at just the right level was difficult so I hope I have got it right for you.

I always try to carefully structure the courses I deliver so that one topic links to the next topic. This book is the same, it tells a story and the best way to read it initially is from beginning to end, so find a few hours, get a drink and settle back and enjoy. After you have read it once I hope it will become an old friend that you will revisit time and again as a source of reference. To aid its usefulness as a reference book there is a simple memory aid covering some of the key elements of coaching and learner centred approaches as Appendix C.

The book is designed around the same learner centred and coaching principles it advocates. It looks first at the problem and then at possible solutions, it asks you questions that I hope it will encourage you to ask questions of yourself.

As you will read later, I do not advocate a single approach to learning but a mixed approach. In this book I focus on learner centred and coaching approaches, but this does not mean I see these as the only approaches – far from it. As with all learning the skill of the instructor is to identify the best mix of approaches for the learner at that time, based on the learner's needs, preferences and the learning goal to be achieved.

Scope and Terms Used

I have, as much as possible, tried to stay away from jargon but I have had to use some terms that need to be clearly defined and understood. Where these terms are used I have tried to define them as clearly as I possibly can.

Within this book I use the term learner but it is important to recognise that the term learner does not necessarily mean a learner driver, it simply means someone who is there to develop – we are all, or should be, learners. The techniques and practices discussed in this book can be used perfectly well with both learner and experienced drivers.

To make the reading a pleasant experience I have not referenced the book in the classic way but I have included a bibliography at the end and where I would normally reference a piece of text I have placed a number to highlight that the authors can be found in the bibliography.

2. Background

Just like any instructor, I have a unique view of driver education based on my own experience and many hours of discussion with driving instructors from all over the UK and Europe. In these discussions 3 themes tend to emerge.

The first is that driving instructors feel they do a good job and that when their drivers go for test they are well prepared and able to drive but once passed their test some, by no means all, seem to forget much of what they had learned and drive in a way the instructor never advocated.

The second theme to emerge, particularly in the UK, is that due to the recession and other factors running a driving school is difficult and developing a strong and sustainable business is a challenge.

The final theme is that the instructors gain tremendous enjoyment from their role and see self-development as a way of further increasing both their enjoyment and improving their business.

If you ask yourself why you are reading this book I suspect your answer will fall somewhere within the three themes outlined above. Therefore, the next question is 'how does coaching and learner centred approaches to driver education link to these themes'?

Well, these approaches:

Aim to make those you teach safer by enhancing their own abilities to solve problems and learn from their experience - the road safety benefit

Increase your own satisfaction levels – happy instructors lead to happy learners

Increase the satisfaction levels of those you coach – leads to increased number of client referrals

Whilst I am a great advocate of coaching and learner centred approaches I do live in the real world, coaching is not a cure-all. It is a tool to be used and mixed with other techniques and, if used well, it is a tool that offers you a great deal and one I am sure you will find highly beneficial.

But what are learner centred and coaching techniques? I have read many books on the subject and I have never really found a clear answer, most definitions offer an outcome rather than a clear definition. The definition I prefer for driver education is simply this, **coaching and learner centred approaches aim, as much as possible, to make the learner both the learner and the teacher**[1]. I will return and expand on this definition later.

3. Education -vs- Training
Within the driver training industry there is a great deal of debate about the use of coaching and learner centred approaches and how these approaches differ from instruction. Before the benefits of these approaches can be fully understood it is useful to fully appreciate the causal factors associated with crash involvement.

Why do so many newly qualified drivers crash?
Novice drivers crash for many reasons but let us start with looking at a very simple crash scenario.

> A newly qualified driver is involved in a collision whilst out with 3 friends. The time of the incident is 11.15pm and it occurred on the approach to a roundabout. The driver collided with the rear of the car in front.

There could be many reasons for this collision but they could be placed broadly under 4 headings:

> Personality
> Journey
> Reading the road
> Vehicle skills

Personality issues could include such things as peer pressure, thrill seeking, poor levels of concentration, self-image, emotional state, etc. These traits and predispositions would be influenced by the context in which the **journey** took place.

Context of the journey is a term used to describe the purpose of the journey, where we are going, who we are with, if there are time pressures associated with the journey, time of day, etc. The context of the journey may influence how we behave, for example, if the driver was easily influenced by peer pressure having friends in the car could increase the likelihood of the driver showing off. These journey-related issues could easily affect the driver's attention and judgements, increasing the demand related to **reading the road.** It is also possible that peer influence may lead the driver to accept smaller gaps in traffic and to approach situations at a faster speed than they would normally do. These increased speeds and decreased safety margins increase the demand the driver is placing on their **vehicle skills.**

This example demonstrates that the driver's own personality is one of the key issues. Whilst I am not suggesting that a driving instructor can change someone's personality, it is relatively simple to help someone gain an understanding of how their personality may influence their decisions. However to be able to achieve this, the driver needs to be able to **self-evaluate** their own performance and consider how the influences just discussed may affect their judgments and the choices they make.

Self-evaluation in driving is a process by which a person is able to monitor their own performance, to identify areas of learning, to analyse how to use this new learning and to develop a plan of improvement.

The need to self-evaluate is a critical skill a driver needs to have post-test as without it learning from experience can be a slow and even a dangerous process [2]. The concept of self-evaluation is discussed in detail in section 8.

This is where learner centred and coaching approaches become vital. These approaches focus not just on developing the learner's current performance but on the development of their own self-evaluation skills. They encourage the learner to consider not just what is happening now, in a driving lesson, but to identify barriers that would prevent them deploying the skills and knowledge they gain in training to real journeys in the future. Learner centred approaches look to reduce some of the fundamental bars to **deep learning**.

Deep learning is a term to describe when the learning belongs to the learner and used by them as part of their normal behaviour. Often in driver training the learning that takes place is superficial, in other words the learner will behave in a way advocated by the instructor, but once the instructor presence is no longer there, after the driving test for example, the learner will drive in the way they feel is correct and is in line with their personal picture of a good driver.

Dr Diane Parker and Professor Steve Stradling in 2001[3] suggested that drivers learn to drive in three distinct phases. They termed these as:

Technical Mastery: in this phase of driver development the unqualified driver learns how to move, stop and steer the vehicle.

Reading the Road: the unqualified driver develops the hazard perception skills required to integrate in the traffic environment.

Expressive Phase: this phase refers to how a driver gives expression to their personality, attitudes and motivations through their driving.

An example of this Expressive phase would be a driver who believes that they would impress their friends by driving quickly. In training with the instructor present this is unlikely to manifest itself and if it did the instructor would quickly stop the behaviour. However, once free of this control the behaviour could reappear.

As shown in this example this final phase of driver development is rarely seen by a driving instructor at the pre-test level as the personality that controls the car in pre-test training is almost certainly the **driving instructor's**. This is true in two ways:

The instructor will intervene in the driving process if the learner driver attempts to drive in a manner not compatible with the driving style being taught by the instructor.

The pupil, motivated by the desire to be put forward by the instructor for the driving test, will accept the social model being advocated by the instructor.

Therefore the internal picture the driver has is only fully seen once the driver is free from the instructor and is able to express it. This internal picture is the driver's own view of what good driving is and how a good driver behaves. It is based on their experience to date and on the goals they are trying to achieve when driving the vehicle. These goals are almost certainly to get from A to B safely but may include other sub-goals, such as impressing a friend, arriving on time, gaining a thrill, etc.

3.1 The Goals for Driver Education

In the opening section of the book I hope I made the case for **expanding driver training to become driver education**. So what is the difference? Well, driver training tends to focus on the ability of the driver to handle the vehicle and to integrate with traffic. Driver education extends this to cover a range of topics as outlined in the Goals for Driver Education (GDE Matrix) (Keskinen et al, 2010)[4]as shown in Table One.

Level	Knowledge and skills	Risk increasing factors	Self-evaluation
Level V Social Environmental	Culture, legislation, enforcement, sub-cultures, social groups, group values and norms	Little or no understanding of how cultural / sub-cultural issues impact on driving.	How culture/ impacts on driving decisions / judgements
Level IV Goals for life and skills for living	Lifestyle, age, group, culture, social position etc. v.s driving behaviour	Sensation seeking, group norms, peer pressure	Introspective competence, own preconditions, impulse control
Level III Goals and context of driving	Modal choice, choice of time, role of motives, route planning	Alcohol, fatigue, low friction, rush hours, young passengers	Own motives influencing choices, self-critical thinking
Level II Driving in traffic	Traffic rules, cooperation, hazard perception, Automation	Disobeying rules, tailgating, low friction, vulnerable road users	Calibration of driving skills, own driving style
Level I Vehicle control	Car functioning, protection systems, vehicle control, physical laws	No seatbelts, breakdown of vehicle system, worn-out tyres	Calibration of car control skills

Table 1: Keskinen et al (2010) Goals for Driver Education (GDE) 5 – SOC Matrix

4. Why Use Coaching in Driver Education?

Many of the risk increasing factors listed in the first four levels as identified in the Goals for Driver Education fall into two broad categories of age and experience.

Age: During adolescence major changes take place in the structure of the brain. This process is called maturation. The process starts at the back of the brain and works forwards meaning the front part of the brain is the last to fully mature. This front part of the brain is thought to control a number of key functions linked to driving, including impulse control, visual search, self-evaluation, planning and risk management. You can use coaching approaches to raise the awareness of young people as to how and when age related issues may influence their driving decisions and help them to develop coping strategies to address these issues.

Frequently, driver training tends to be limited to errors committed by the learner whilst driving. Coaching offers the opportunity to encourage the learner driver to consider how they will react in post-test situations. This is achieved by encouraging the learner to consider how behaviour is influenced by different contexts. For example, how their driving may be influenced by time and / or peer influences. The aim is to assist the learner to identify their own strengths and weaknesses and in so doing become increasingly more aware of themselves. These approaches are discussed in much more depth in section 8.

Experience: You cannot put an old head on a young person's shoulders but you **can** develop a person's ability to learn more effectively from their own experiences. Learning from experience is a natural process but it is also a process that can be accelerated and refined. Without this refinement learning from experience can even be counterproductive.
But what do I mean by experience? Well, experience is generally seen as being related to car skills and dealing with traffic. However, in reality it is much more than this. What about the experience of dealing with car skills and dealing with traffic and time pressures? What about the experience of

navigating, dealing with time pressures, dealing with traffic and car skills? What about the experience of dealing with time pressures, navigation, fatigue, peer pressure, dealing with traffic and car skills? So experience is much wider than simply handling the vehicle in traffic, it is related to the driving task in its entirety. Developing someone's ability to learn from their experience should be one of the most important goals for a driving instructor. It is impossible to teach a driver everything and how to deal with every traffic situation they will ever face. Drivers need to be able to learn quickly from the experience so they can develop without the instructors help.

Of course the danger with learning from experience is that the wrong lessons can be drawn from the experience. Imagine a driver who is in a rush and follows too closely to the vehicle in front but nothing happens – they get away with it. What lesson would be learnt here? It is very possible that they will draw the conclusion that this driving behaviour is OK and poses few dangers to them. You only need to watch the following distances on a motorway and note the number of drivers who are comfortable following closely behind the vehicle in front – they have learnt this through their own experience. But has this been good learning?

The question is not if we learn from experience but if we learn the right things from our experiences. The quality of the learning is linked to our ability to engage and analyse the experiences we have. Coaching strongly focuses on the development of the skills needed to engage and learn from experience, in other words the ability of the learner to self-evaluate, by placing a much greater emphasis on the learner's ability to identify, analyse and develop. Increasingly the development of a learner's self-evaluation skills is being seen as a critical element in driver education.

To assist the learner to develop these skills the coach needs to recognise and know how to reduce two significant barriers to learning, namely **resistance** and **anxiety**.

4.1 Previous Learning and Resistance

We start learning about traffic early on in our life, from an early stage we are watching traffic, being driven in cars and learning what is acceptable behaviour and what is not. By the time we come to drive a vehicle at the age of 17 in the UK we will have a strongly fixed view of what a good driver is and how a good driver behaves. This view of driving will be internal to ourselves, is likely to be hidden from others who we feel may not share this view, and will influence the way we interpret the driving environment.

This picture of a good driver will be based on many things including:

> How our parents drove and dealt with traffic as pedestrians
> Being a passenger in a vehicle
> Our own experience of being a pedestrian
> The view we believe is advocated by our peer group
> The influence of the media
> Personal beliefs about how to behave, both on the road and in our lives generally

This previous knowledge and experience means that everything we are told about driving will be filtered or interpreted against and through this personal picture of a good driver. This interpretation will mean that many of the messages delivered by an instructor will be seen as unimportant, re-constructed or even rejected. Many instructors will see this on a daily basis, for example a learner may ask an instructor who is driving them out to a quiet area "Do you always drive like this?" This question may indicate the driving being demonstrated does not fit with the learner's personal picture of a driver. This personal picture frequently leads to resistance, with the learner nodding in all the right places but not necessarily altering their core beliefs about what a good driver is or how a good driver should behave. Of course this is a very negative view of previous knowledge. It can also be very positive as not all the previous knowledge will be poor or in conflict with safe driving. The challenge for the instructor is to help the learner to understand how this previous knowledge can influence behaviour and their own strengths and weaknesses.

4.2 Anxiety

When we learn something there are a number of questions that interfere with our ability to learn. These questions tend to be negative and raise our levels of anxiety, the more anxious we become the more difficult it is for us to learn. Common types of questions include:

> Will I be successful?
> Does my instructor think I am stupid?
> Can I do this?
> Will learning this be worthwhile?
> Am I making progress?
> Will I crash the car?
> This is dangerous and I could die?
> Are my friends better at this than me?
> I never find learning things easy?
> If I drive like this how will my peers view me?

All these questions increase our concerns, distract us and build barriers to success. These questions can almost become so loud to us that we struggle to listen and focus on the information being delivered to us.

The role of the coach therefore is to create a learning environment which reduces anxiety. We will discuss how this can be achieved later in this book.

5. Coaching – What is it?

As I have already indicated earlier in this book defining coaching is not as simple as it may first sound. One of the difficulties is that there are many overlaps between what could be called instruction and what could be called coaching and there are many different forms of each. Coaching and learner centred approaches use many of the techniques used in instruction and this leads many instructors to believe they are already coaching. Therefore the difference is perhaps one of focus.

Hermes, a 3 year EU-funded Project, looking at how coaching could be used in driver education, defined coaching as:

> **Coaching is a learner centred approach that engages body, mind, and emotions to develop inner and outer awareness and responsibility through an equal relationship between the learner and coach.** HERMES 2010

This is quite a complex statement so it is worth spending a few minutes unpacking it.

5.1 Learner Centred

Learner centred is a term which is often closely linked with the term coaching and I see little to separate them. Learner centred and coaching is about placing the learner at the **centre** of the learning process. This is much more than simply structuring or developing a set of lessons for a specific learner's needs. **It is also about making the learner, as much as possible, their own teacher through the development of their own self-evaluation skills.**

5.2 Relationship

This is the most vital element of coaching. The relationship should be **one of equals** where the learner and coach work closely together. The aim of the coach should be to help the learner learn through the reduction and removal of the learning barriers as outlined in the previous section of this book.

As previously discussed one of the main learning bars is anxiety. For this reason one of the critical elements of the coach / learner relationship is the need for the coach to be **non-judgemental.** This often surprises instructors with instructors responding in one of two ways. The first is: 'I am the instructor and I need to judge my pupil's performance'. The other response is: 'I give lots of praise so I am not judgemental'. In reality these are the same side of the coin. **In coaching the aim is to help the learner to learn how to judge their own performance**. A number of techniques

that will help you achieve this will be discussed later in this book.
Being non-judgemental is also vitally important in reducing the other bar
to learning we have discussed, resistance. As previously discussed this
resistance comes from the conflict between the learner's internal picture of
a good driver and the new information being presented. Building a strong
non- judgemental relationship with a learner will help the learner to explore
these conflicts in a more relaxed and constructive environment, rather than
the learner hiding them away from the view of the coach. The relationship
is looked at in more depth in section 6.

5.3 Awareness and responsibility

Over the past decade education has placed greater importance on the
development of the learner's ability to self-evaluate their own performance.
If you are not able to identify for yourself where you need to improve you
cannot be fully aware, and it therefore follows that if you are not aware
you cannot be fully responsible. **One of the main aims of coaching
is to increase a learner's level of awareness and responsibility, and
the development of self-evaluation skills is a critical element in this
process.** To be fully self-aware you not only need to be aware of your
actions but aware of the physical and emotional states that will influence
your decision making process. A coach therefore needs to not only
encourage the learner to consider their observed behaviour but also
to consider the physical and emotional aspects of the decision making
process.

Against this background the HERMES definition of:

> **Coaching is a learner centred approach that engages body,
> mind, and emotions to develop inner and outer awareness and
> responsibility through an equal relationship between the
> learner and coach**. HERMES 2010

is starting to make a great deal more sense than perhaps it did when you
first read it.

6. Building the Relationship

This is the most critical element of coaching. To be effective the relationship must be non-judgemental. But what does this really mean?

6.1 A non-judgemental relationship

Coaching is about encouraging the learner to think about and explore their own understanding of the world. This understanding is unlikely to be the same as the coach's but it will be very real to the learner. In order for the learner to reflect on their reality and develop through reflection they must feel able to say what they think, feel and believe. This is very difficult and will only be achieved in a situation where they do not feel judged. Of course, we judge people when we give them both negative and positive feedback so you may now be thinking 'how do I do this if both positive and negative feedback is wrong?'

The key to this is to create an environment where the learners assess themselves, and this is achieved by the use of questions that encourage the learner to consider their actions from a number of perspectives. For example, asking a learner "Is there anything you feel you could improve?" is non-judgemental. What you have simply asked them to do is to forward their own judgement of their performance. The question is also worded positively using 'improve' as this reduces the judgemental aspect as most people accept that, even if they feel they have successfully completed something, there could be room for further improvement.

The main criticism of this is that whenever you ask a learner a question they presume you have identified a fault and therefore simply by asking them a question you are judging them.

This is only correct if the learner has been conditioned into this response by only being asked questions when something did go wrong. The use of positive reinforcement is a critical tool in any coach's toolbox. **Asking a learner to reflect when they have driven well is just as important, and in many ways more important, than correcting faults.** Reflecting on positive events helps to confirm this action in the learner's mind enabling them to build a realistic level of **confidence**.

Over confidence is regularly cited as an issue associated with novice driver crash involvement and is frequently linked to poor calibration of driving ability, in other words the learner believes they are better than they really are. Coaching aims to **increase the learner's self-evaluations skills** and, in so doing, help the learner to have a more realistic calibration of their driving.

6.2 Qualities of a good coach[6]
What qualities does a coach need? One way to identify these qualities is to try and imagine a person who made you feel special when you were young. What qualities did they have? The person I would choose would be Gramps (my grandfather.) He made me feel special as he:

> Had time for me
> Believed in my ability to succeed
> Treated me as an equal
> Listened to my views
> Asked me questions about my views
> Encouraged me to believe in myself
> Was never flustered
> Was fun
> Was honest with me
> Didn't make me feel judged

The list above would describe an excellent coach and it is exactly these qualities that a coach needs to possess. Try and think of someone who influenced you far longer than the contact you had with them, this could be a grandparent, a teacher, youth worker, etc. Think about the qualities they had. Try to imagine what you would need to do so that one day in the future when someone asks one of your learners 'who was one of the most influential people in your life?' they will say – 'oh, my driving instructor!'

6.3 EQ – Building Rapport

To build this type of open and honest relationship requires the coach to have excellent levels of emotional intelligence (EQ). Emotional Intelligence is a term used to describe a person's awareness of their own and another's emotions and their ability to adapt their responses appropriately to gain a favourable outcome. Figure 1 shows a simple diagram of the three strands of Emotional Intelligence.

Figure 1: Emotional Intelligence, Based on Passmore., J. University of East London Coaching for Driver Development: University of East London.

How we feel influences the way in which we interact with others, for example if we are worried or even euphoric, we can easily become distracted. This is communicated to the other person as a lack of interest and quickly picked up through our body language. High levels of EQ start with a high level of personal awareness. Understanding yourself and understanding how your emotions may influence your learner's performance, or how you interpret their words and actions, is vital. If your outlook is negative then your learner will quickly pick up on this and may perform negatively. Of course the opposite is also true; if your learner's emotions are not conducive to the task this can negatively influence you.

The key to EQ is to be aware of your own emotional state, your learner's and to be able to modify your own behaviour to maximise the benefits of the relationship. Building and establishing rapport is vital in the coaching relationship. Rapport is building a trusting harmonious relationship based on mutual respect and, most importantly, acceptance that both the coach and learner are equals.

Of course the instructor has the technical knowledge and in this respect is the expert. However, if the coach is to encourage the learner to engage with the knowledge on a deep rather than superficial level the coach has to understand the learner's own internal view of driving. The only person who knows this internal view is the learner, so the learner is also the expert in this regard.

If the relationship is not one of equals this can result in a number of problems, most notably the learner will simply conform to the behaviour the instructor advocates but without really seeing it as fitting with their internal picture of a good driver; often hiding this personal picture away from the instructor. This means that once the instructor's controlling influence is removed the driver will drive in the way that they feel fits with them. The aim for a coach is not to simply enforce behaviour whilst they are present but to assist the learner to become aware and responsible for their own future behaviour.

6.4 Active listening

There are a number of skills required by the coach to build this type of relationship, and they are generally grouped together under the term of active listening. There are many elements to active listening including:

Watching
Matching
Repeating
Construct analysis
Reflection

6.5 Watching

We communicate as much by non-verbal means as we do by voice. Therefore, actively listening starts there - what clues is the learner giving about their mood and feelings? Do you get the feeling they are bright and breezy today or down and out? Looking at someone walking towards the car, how they sit, hold the wheel, the amount of eye contact they give are all elements of active listening. So, active listening is much more than simply listening, it is about looking at the learner and asking yourself questions about their body language. Most people can pick up the obvious clues but a good coach can quickly pick up on the less obvious and more hidden clues. Key areas to watch include:

Body posture: are they relaxed or tense? Is the body posture backing up what they say or at odds with it?
Levels of eye contact: is this more or less what you expect from this learner?

Facial expressions: what is the face saying? Have a look at http://face.paulekman.com/default.aspx for more information.
Gestures: are these relaxed and fluent or stiff and stilted?

All of these are clues to the learner's feelings and emotions but to read them well you will need to really know the learner and you also have to understand the culture they come from. All I can do here is to alert you to the importance of watching. Of course, you need to remember that they are also watching you!

6.6 Matching

A good way to build rapport is to match your learner. Matching is about trying to make your learner feel at ease by matching their body language, tone of voice, levels of eye contact, etc. Remember rapport is about a relationship of equals and this would be difficult to achieve if the coach is dominating the proceedings by use of strong body language.

6.7 Repeating

Showing an interest in what the learner says is not always as easy as it sounds; the key word here is showing. If you simply listen how will the learner know you are interested? Repeating is a great way of engaging the learner and showing you are listening. It consists of repeating a short part of the conversation. When done well the learner will quickly start to share more of their thoughts.

> **Coach:** How are you today?
> **Learner:** Great – thanks, had a good day at school.
> **Coach:** A good day at school?
> **Learner:** Yes, I won a prize for some art I entered in a competition
> **Coach:** Some art?
> **Learner:** Yes, I never told you have I but I do art in my spare time...

6.8 Construction

Active listening is not always just hearing the words, it is also listening for the real meaning. Often we construct a discussion to hide areas of ourselves we do not wish others to know about. For example:

> Your learner sees a car about to pull away from the side of the road but fails to react. When you ask about the situation your learner says: 'If we had crashed that would have been the other driver's fault not mine.'

Construction is a process by which the coach considers what the learner has really said. In this case the learner has said they would see the fault being with the other driver, but there could be several other underlying messages that may give a clue to the learner's beliefs about driving. Their reply could indicate one or more of the following:

> That driving is about fault
> That there would be no negative consequences to them as a result of a collision
> Having a collision is OK if it is not your fault
> Driving is about following the rules no matter what the consequences

Whilst none of the above statements was actually said, they could be inferred from what was said. This type of listening is critical as it would allow the coach to help the learner to explore much more than the words alone conveyed.

6.9 Reflection
This approach is similar to repeating but looks to check understanding of what has been said. It also gives the added benefit of allowing the learner to hear what they have said from another perspective. An example of this would be if a learner said something like:

> **Learner:** That driver took a big risk pulling out in front of me at that junction.
> **Coach:** That is interesting, are you saying there was no risk to you?

Here the coach has simply reflected back what the learner has said from a different perspective and, in so doing, has helped the learner to hear more clearly an alternative meaning. Of course a coach would need to develop this further but this offers a great opener to a deeper conversation. This type of challenging reflection would need to be introduced only when a good level of rapport has been established.

7. The Toolbox

In this section we will look at the basic tools used in coaching.

7.1 Using Questions

As you are already beginning to see, one of the main tools in a coach's toolbox is the use of questions. In coaching, questions are not just used to test knowledge and understanding but are used to encourage **self-reflection** by the learner. To do this effectively the questions need to be open rather than closed or leading.

A closed question is a question that requires a specific answer or a number of specific answers, 'yes or no' questions or questions such as 'what does a red traffic light mean?'

An example of a leading question is below:

> 'Do you think you were a bit fast down that road?'

This question is very leading as it immediately points the learner to an issue to be considered and pretty much points them to the answer. It is also judgemental, as it does not offer the learner the opportunity to consider if they had driven at the correct speed.

I am not saying that these would never be used but where possible the coach should ask open questions that maximise reflection. Typical questions used when coaching a driving session could include:

> 'Is there anything you would like to improve on the last part of the drive?'

> 'Can you describe what happened?'

> 'What were you feeling there?'

These questions are open and place the learner in the active role of developing their own knowledge through learning to solve their own problems and self-evaluating their own performance. A good test of an open question is to ask yourself if you could answer that question - if you can't, it is generally open. These types of questions tend to start with:

> What do you feel...
> What do you think...
> What is your opinion...
> Why do you feel...

You might know what you would like to hear but you can't say what someone knows, thinks or feels or what their opinion is. These questions encourage self-reflection and are not judgemental as there is no wrong or right answer – simply the learner's answer.

Of course it takes time to think and/or work through a problem or question. How do you respond to a difficult question? Do you repeat it in your own mind? Then think about your reply? How long does this take? **Remember your learner needs this time also, so don't rush in, let them have time to consider the question and their answer. You need to have confidence that your learner will come up with the answer.**

7.2 Problem solving
Driving is all about problem solving, related to 'how do I drive from A to B safely?' However, there are lots of sub-problems to solve along the way. **It is therefore one of the primary roles of a coach to help a learner to develop their problem solving skills.**

To do this the coach needs to present the learner with a problem to solve. Let us consider how most driving instructors have been taught to instruct. For the sake of this example imagine you are about to teach a left turn from a main road to a minor road. You have arrived at the junction and you are about to brief your learner. What would your briefing start with? In most cases this is likely to start with the identification of the junction and then move to MSMPSL. This approach is presenting a solution, but has the learner really identified the problem that this solution is attempting to solve? If not, then it can be very difficult for the learner to readily grasp the solution. A coaching approach would be more likely to start with the problem and work through to a solution together. A mind mapping exercise could be used for example.

7.3 Mind mapping

An alternative approach to the left turn briefing would be to ask the learner to mind map what they see are the dangers associated with a left turn. Even a learner who has never turned left before will be able to provide a comprehensive list of dangers. The mind map below is a typical example

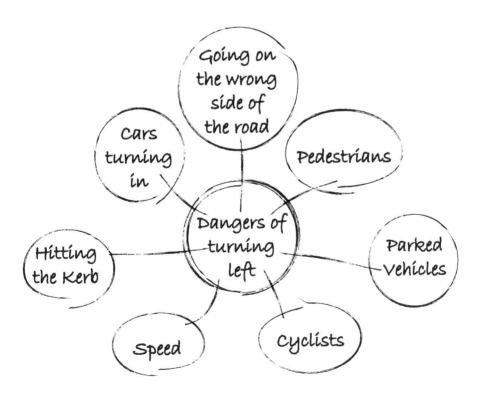

This map is based on a similar one that I did with my 14 year old son. He easily provided the answers, even though he has never been behind the wheel of a car.

This mind mapping approach is excellent as it:

> Helps the learner to clearly identify the problem they are trying to solve
> Assists the coach to identify the concerns the learner has with regards to the issue
> Provides a readymade training aid for the learner to take away from the session
> May reveal the learner's inner picture of good driving

Once the learner has focused on the problem to be solved the solutions become much clearer and easier to grasp. Mind mapping in this way is a very useful tool as it may offer the coach invaluable insights into behaviour that mere observation may fail to identify.

An instructor who attended one of our instructor workshops provided feedback with a brilliant example based on a left turn exercise. When asking the learner to mind map the dangers of turning left the learner said: "Looking like a learner". This immediately highlighted a potential issue and explained the learner's reluctance to slow down on the approach on the initial attempts. Rather than wasting time discussing the use of brakes etc. the instructor was able to move directly to the root of the issue, which was the learner's concern about looking like a learner, and quickly helped the learner to address the issue and develop. This is a great illustration and links to another way in which this type of mind mapping technique could be used.

We have all come across learners who have really struggled for some reason. Often this difficulty is linked to previous knowledge or the learner being very anxious for some reason. Asking a learner to mind map the difficulty can help in both instances as it allows the learner to offer their thoughts about the issue in a non-judgemental way, while helping to throw light on a hidden difficulty. Speed choice, for example, is often an issue that drivers struggle with, and asking a driver to identify all the things upon which they base their speed choices can open up many new areas of discussion thus allowing the coach and learner to identify hidden concerns that may be influencing performance.

7.4 Scenarios

One of the most important aspects of driving is the context in which the journey takes place. For example, where are you going? Who are you with? Is the journey time constrained? What is your state of mind? All these things will influence our judgements and therefore our behaviour.

Presenting a scenario can help the learner to consider how they would react in future situations. For example, I frequently ask driving instructors what an amber light means. They immediately give the text book answer along the lines of 'stop, unless you cannot do so safely'. However, the next question usually results in some raised eyes to the ceiling. What does an amber traffic light mean if you are late to pick a pupil up for a pre-test driving lesson? Many in the audience then mumble something like: "You can get through before red!"

This simple scenario is an excellent example of how you can encourage someone to reflect on how their own personality, beliefs, and journey context can influence their driving decisions. Some people are very laid back about being late and would just think I will be there when I get there. Others believe being late is unacceptable, and others would be influenced by what they saw as the urgency of the situation. Understanding how you would react in this type of situation is the first step in developing effective coping strategies. The use of scenarios is discussed in more detail in section 12

7.5 Case Studies

There are many ways to use a case study but probably the most effective is when the opportunity presents itself during a coaching session. Imagine that you are driving down the road and both you and the learner identify a red car approaching from a side road to your left. The driver of the red car looks quickly at you and then pulls out. Your learner reacts well and in a timely fashion to the incident. This is a great case study you can use to encourage the learner to consider a number of issues.

> **Coach:** What did you feel about that?
> **Learner:** Fine, I could tell they were going to pull out.
> **Coach:** How could you tell?
> **Learner:** The speed and the way they quickly looked.
> **Coach:** Why do you think they were driving like that?
> **Learner:** They were in a rush.
> **Coach:** So you felt they were in a rush?
> **Learner:** Yes
> **Coach:** Can you think of a time when you might be in a rush?
> **Learner:** Yes, I could be late for college.
> **Coach:** How do you feel being late for college could influence your driving?
> **Learner:** Oh, I could rush I suppose?
> **Coach:** What thing could you do to deal with those pressures?
> **Learner:** I would ignore them – I would just have to be late.
> **Coach:** That's interesting, is there anything else you could do if you found it difficult to ignore the time pressure.
> **Learner:** Oh, I could...

I have stopped the discussion there but the coach would go on and explore possible coping strategies. What is interesting in the discussion was that the coach used the initial incident as a way of developing the learner's own awareness of how those types of pressure could influence them in the future. I refer to this as the **switch**, people are usually quite happy to comment on others and in this situation the learner was delighted to do so. The learning however became more powerful when the learner was encouraged to consider how they would react in a similar situation.

It was also interesting to note how the coach did not allow the discussion to stop when the learner offered a poor strategy of 'Oh, I would ignore them.' This can be very hard to do but is frequently offered as a solution. The coach dealt with this well by encouraging the learner to think past this to a situation where the ignoring strategy failed by using an options question. We discuss this approach of using options questions in greater depth in section 10.3.

7.6 The Learning Investment – Ownership

Who has ownership of the ideas and concepts you teach? You may already be thinking.... you, society, the learner. **In the end it must be the learner - they need to really feel they have ownership of the idea and concepts.** If they don't why would they apply them after you leave the vehicle for the last time?

So how do you encourage the learner to have ownership of these ideas, concepts and ultimately their behaviour? This is a very difficult question but one approach is using what I term **a learning investment**.

Frequently something you have earned through hard work can have a much greater personal value than something given freely. For this reason you should always try and encourage the learner to work hard at developing and refining their own ideas. In other words, solving their own problems. Problem solving requires the learner to work hard to develop solutions and therefore **invest** effort and take ownership of their **learning**.

Frequently the driving instructor provides information that, with a little imagination and work, the learner could have worked out for themselves. Simply receiving knowledge places the learner in a passive role in the learning process and, just like a free CD in a newspaper, sometimes a gift has less meaning than something you have had to work hard to achieve. **The aim of an instructor therefore should be, as much as**

possible, to place the learner in the active role of producing their own knowledge[7]. In this way the learner has to work to gain knowledge, and this effort leads the learner to attach greater value to the knowledge they have **earned**.

I am not saying that the instructor providing an answer is always wrong, but it is important for the instructor to clearly understand the reasons why they have taken that option. Often we do this as we don't want to make learning a hard process and we are nice people so why not lend a helping hand. However, we can be too kind and in doing so we retain the ownership of the knowledge we want to pass on.

8. Self-evaluation

We all learn from experience but the quality and the speed of the learning process is reliant on the ability of the driver to **engage** with the process. The coach's role is to help the learner to maximise this learning process by helping them to develop their ability to critically analyse their driving. In other words, the learner must be able to self-evaluate their own performance. It is important that this skill is developed both with regards to negative behaviour and positive behaviour. Learning from positives helps to reinforce this behaviour but frequently instructors are too focused at identifying faults. The testing system in the UK is a fault-based system, however, there is no reason that this fault based system should be the only focus in a driving lesson.

8.1 A Model of Self-evaluation[8]

Self-evaluation could be viewed as 4 overlapping stages consisting of:

> Self-monitoring
> Self-analysis
> Self-identification
> Self-development

Whilst we consider each stage in turn, it is important to remember that to be effective the self-evaluation process must be a continuous one, as

38

outlined in Figure 2. It is also necessary to recognise that for self-evaluation to be successful the driver must not only be able to self-evaluate their own driving performance at the time of the event, but also any possible influence that their emotions, life goals, journey goals, etc. had on their performance.

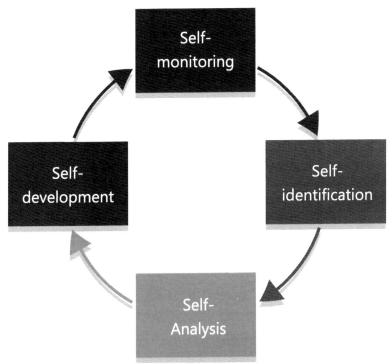

Figure 2: A Model of Self –evaluation, Edwards (2010)

8.1.1 Self-monitoring

Self-monitoring is the first element of the self-evaluation process, and within this stage the driver should be monitoring their own performance with the aim of identifying any **'learning triggers'** that may occur.

A learning trigger is any event which does not fit with the driver's previous experience, or which offers an opportunity for further learning to take place. In order for the next stage, self-identification, to be effective the learner must have a clear internal picture of what they are attempting to achieve whilst driving and be able to monitor their own driving performance against this picture.

8.1.2 Self-identification
The term 'learning trigger' as used in this model is highly descriptive of the process as their occurrence needs to trigger the driver to move from the self-monitoring stage to an active state of self-analysis. This may not be possible at the time due to other task demands but the event must be logged by the driver and analysed as soon as it is safe. One way in which a coach could help a learner to identify learning triggers is to encourage the learner to develop a personal list of such events during training. These events could include: having to brake harshly or steer suddenly, being taken by surprise by the presence of another road user, a near collision, the successful negotiation of a difficult situation, dealing with a novel situation, etc.

8.1.3 Self-analysis
Once the driver has successfully identified a learning trigger the driver needs to be able to critically analyse the event and identify a **number** of possible solutions, or coping strategies. It is important, where possible, that the driver considers a number of options rather than a single option, as the obvious option may not be the best when compared to other possible solutions. The self-analysis process should not be limited to actual events but should also include the driver considering if their emotional state, life goals, journey goals, etc. had influenced their judgements.

8.1.4 Self-development
Once a number of options have been identified the driver should then be able to select the option they feel is most appropriate to implement in their future driving behaviour. Once implemented they should then start the process of self-monitoring their driving with the view of assessing whether the new strategy has been successful and to identify further learning triggers as they occur.

8.2 Developing Self-evaluation as a Skill

There are many ways a coach could help the development of a driver's own self-assessment skills using the self-evaluation model outlined previously. A simple example is below:

8.2.1 Self-monitoring and identification

The coach asks the driver what they think is meant by the term 'self-evaluation'. Once agreed the instructor introduces the concept of learning triggers and encourages the learner to develop a list of personal learning triggers. Once these learning triggers have been identified by the learner the coach could ask the learner to drive and monitor their own performance with the aim of identifying when a learning trigger has occurred.

8.2.2 Self-analysis and development

Once a learning trigger has occurred, and ideally been identified by the driver, the coach should ask the learner to suggest a number of options to prevent the situation occurring again, or how they could incorporate a positive learning trigger in their future driving. These options should be carefully considered with both the benefits and negatives being clearly identified and discussed. Once the possible options have been discussed the driver should be asked which of the possible options could be incorporated in their driving.

Within the outline above it is necessary for the coach to have a very clear understanding that the aim is to maximise the learner's own self-evaluation skills not simply correcting any errors that had occurred.

8.3 Feedback

One of the most effective forms of feedback is self-feedback. The role of the coach is to encourage the learner to consider what they have done and develop their own view of this. However, this does not mean that a coach in driver education does not give feedback but the key is to encourage the learner to consider the issue first.

An example of the importance of this approach occurred when I was on my Continued Ability and Fitness to Instruct test (Check test) some years ago. Before I go into this I would like to highlight that I am using this as an example as, on the debrief, it is one of the rare times when driving instructors are no longer giving but receiving feedback. It is not at all meant to be a critique of the system or a criticism of the examiner conducting the test.

During the check test I had asked the learner a question and had distracted them at a moment we could have pulled out of the road end we were waiting at. Was this a misjudgement on my part or lack of knowledge? We will return to that question in a moment.

At the end of the check-test the examiner said that I succeeded in gaining a grade 6 but that I should not have asked the question at that junction.

This is an example of poor feedback. In that situation the examiner learnt nothing about me. If they had asked if there was anything I felt I could have improved this would have allowed me to show that I had identified the issue myself and would have demonstrated that it was a misjudgement rather than a lack of knowledge. Can I stress here the examiner was excellent and I got on with them very well and it could have simply been a misjudgement on their part on the day. I would need to ask them 'if you were giving that feedback again would there be anything you would do differently?' to know for sure if it was a misjudgement or part of their normal practice.

In telling me my error not only did I feel aggrieved at not being able to give my view initially but it prevented the examiner giving any help I may have needed. They were now unable to know for sure if it was a lack of knowledge or a misjudgement on my part.

Now put yourself in my place, how would you have liked the feedback to have been given? Would you have liked to be told someone else's opinion or asked for yours? Which of these would have increased or decreased anxiety and resistance in you? For me, to be given the opportunity to express my own opinion first is paramount as it:

> Allows the learner to self-identify and offer solutions
> Reduces resistance
> Helps the learner to identify gaps in their knowledge
> Helps the coach and learner to identify the next learning steps

When giving feedback the wording should always be positive. I see little need, if ever, to give negative feedback. You may think I have gone mad with that statement but the important element to this is to ensure that the learner never loses sight of why they are there – to learn. If learning is achieved then there are few events that are not positive. The key therefore is to always view an event as a learning opportunity. Questions that do this include:

> What could you improve next time?
> Is there anything you could do differently next time?
> What do you feel you learnt?

Where the learner is not able to provide self-feedback the coach may have to provide it, but this is rare if the right questions are asked and is likely to be limited to technical knowledge. And this leads me nicely into the question: Can coaching and instruction be mixed?

9. In the mix!

This is probably the most controversial question surrounding coaching. Can we mix it with instruction? Of course this question in itself is an over simplification of the position as there are many approaches to coaching and instruction and many of the approaches overlap. So, I can only answer it in very general terms. My answer is simple –

Yes, but as a general rule coaching comes first!

What I mean by this is that the coach should always try to place the learner in the learner and teaching role and only give the information / answers when the learner recognises the need for further knowledge. In other words the learner wants to draw upon the coach's knowledge in the same way you might use an internet search engine to find the answer to a problem you have identified.

Imagine an example where the learner is too close to the vehicle in front. The coach asks how this could be improved and the learner replies that they should drop back, and immediately does so. The coach then asks, how could you judge the distance? The learner indicates in their answer that they understand the need to see past the vehicle in front and to be able to stop safely but does not have a way of judging it. At this point the coach may wish to offer and explain a solution – the two second rule. So the coach has moved from the coaching to instruction but should, as quickly as possible, return to the coaching role by asking: What advantages do you feel that the 2 second rule I have suggested would offer you? Followed by: What do you think are the disadvantages?

To summarise this approach, you start with coaching but as the focus narrows and the problem is identified by the learner it may be necessary for the coach to offer a technical solution to a specific problem. However, as soon as possible the coach should revert back to coaching. In this way the coach almost becomes the internet search engine. What I mean by this is that the learner has identified the problem, realises they need a solution and draws upon the coach's technical expertise to solve the problem. The important element is that the learner has identified the need for the information and is then encouraged to explore the benefits and disadvantages of the information provided by the coach (Figure 3).

You may now be asking two questions, why explore the disadvantages of the solution and - will this work with everyone? I will return to the first of these questions later in section 10.3 but let's look first at the – 'Will this work for everyone?' question.

Figure 3: The coaching/instruction cycle, Edwards (2010)

9.1 The Need for Energy

The answer is that some will engage readily, others will struggle but probably fewer than you think if you have worked hard to build that all important non-judgemental relationship. The main resistance you will face from the learner is a fear of getting it wrong - anxiety. Once they are confident that they will not be judged it is amazing how their responses grow and they open up. The other resistance is that it is hard work for them. **You are building new connections in the brain as a result of the learning that is taking place and this takes energy – real energy just like running a race.** You need to recognise this and take their energy levels into account in the session.

The other resistance is likely to come from you. It is too easy to get a change in observed behaviour by telling someone what to do but this is likely to be superficial and will not build on the self-evaluation skills so critical to the learner's post-test development.

You will need energy to develop and refine the techniques and approaches outlined in this book and this is not a simple process. You will need the same energy that your learners need. You will probably already know what energises you and what saps your strength. Of course there are some universal truths such as eat well, sleep well, exercise, make time for yourself and love your subject.

There has been a great deal written about the subject of energy so I will not go into it further but you could ask yourself a few questions in order to improve your own energy levels, such as:

On a scale of 1 to 10 with 1 being little or no energy and 10 being full of energy, what would you give yourself today?

Why have you given yourself that number?

What could you do to move that number more towards 10? – try to think of three or four possible actions?

From these options what will you do tomorrow to increase your energy levels?

How will you know if this is successful?

I hope thinking about these questions gave you some ideas. You have also just completed a very simple set of questions that form a model of coaching called GROW.

10. A Coaching Model - GROW
Probably the most well known coaching model is GROW, which I first came across in Sir John Whitmore's book [9]. GROW stands for:

> Goals
> Reality
> Options
> Way forward or what will you do

It is an excellent model for developing performance and comes from Sir John Whitmore's book **Coaching for Performance.**

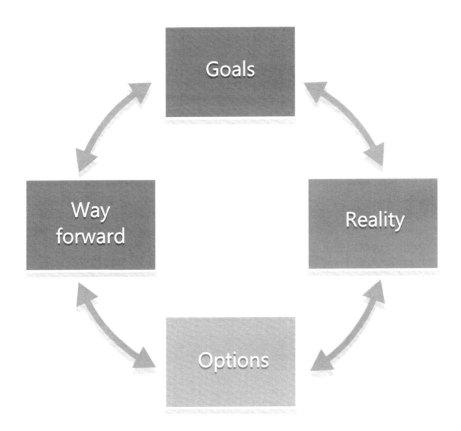

You can use this model to improve a specific area of performance or to plan a session or course of sessions. Of course, however you use it, it is vital that the learner is at the centre of the process.

Many people see the GROW model as linear, however it is probably best viewed as circular and whilst you may wish to start with the GOAL you may find that you may be forced to start at a different point in the cycle. You will also need to move backwards and forwards through the model as new discoveries are made by the learner.

10.1 G for Goals

Setting a goal is an important part of coaching. Goals provide us with something against which we can measure progress and aim to achieve. Getting the goal right can be a challenge, because if the goal is too difficult it can be counterproductive in that it may increase anxiety. If the goal is not sufficiently challenging however, the learner may drop back to be a passive receiver of knowledge rather than the active developer of knowledge.

It becomes even more challenging when I say that where possible the learner should be encouraged to set their own goals. Learning to set goals is an important part of learning how to self-evaluate. The coach must therefore include and maximise the role the learner has in this process by allowing them to practise setting their own goals. **Encouraging the learner to set their own goals helps them to practise analysing their own performance and identifying areas for improvement. Goal setting is a critical part of the development of their self-evaluation skills.**

However, what I am not advocating here is that the coach simply says 'what would you like to do?' in a totally unstructured way. The reality is far from this. Generally a goal should be discussed at the end of the session and linked to something that has been identified as an area for development. Below is a simple example of how this works:

> **Coach:** Based on the session today what would you like to improve next session?
> **Learner:** Well, we discussed junctions and I feel I need to improve them.
> **Coach:** OK, what specifically would you like to improve relating to junctions?
> **Learner:** I'm never sure when to stop.
> **Coach:** Would you like to look at that specific area next week then?
> **Learner:** Please.

Of course this is a simplistic example, and you may find it is never quite as clear cut as this. You may also wish to introduce something new and this can be done easily at this point also.

> **Coach:** OK then, junctions it is. Would you mind if I suggested something also?
> **Learner:** No – not at all
> **Coach:** I would also like to look at a turn in the road, would that be OK, as this is linked to clutch control it may also help you with junctions?
> **Learner:** Yes.

Remember the coaching relationship is a partnership so feel free to add to the goals but do so in a way that adds to the concept of a partnership. **Whenever possible allow the learner to be part of this process, as it is a vital element in the development of their self-evaluation skills.**

Of course, a learner may come out with something completely unexpected, such as: 'I would like to do that really big roundabout.' This possibly would be OK if they had done roundabouts before but it may not be appropriate for the stage of development the learner has reached. This type of goal tells the coach a great deal about the learner. It could be an indication that:

> They are very frightened of this roundabout, or roundabouts generally and cannot think of anything else
> That they have not considered the skills they need to deal with this hazard
> They have very poor self-evaluation skills and do not have a clear picture of their abilities
> They like, or have been taught, to throw themselves in at the deep-end when learning something new.

When this type of goal is suggested by a learner the coach will need to encourage the learner to consider how realistic this is without undermining the learner or judging the goal as being poor. Once again this can be done by use of questions.

> **Coach:** Oh yes, I know the roundabout you mean. What has made you pick that roundabout?
> **Learner:** It is big and fast and there is loads of traffic.
> **Coach:** So are you saying it is very complex?
> **Learner:** Yes it is – very
> **Coach:** What do you feel you could do to work up to that type of roundabout?
> **Learner:** Well, I suppose I need some practice on some simple ones.
> **Coach:** Should we make that the goal for next week so we can work up to the big roundabout?
> **Learner:** Ok.

In this way the coach has maintained the session focus and has assisted the learner to set a realistic goal.

On the next session the coach should always remind the learner of what was agreed as a goal for this session and ensure that the learner has not thought of something else since then. An example of this is outlined below:

> **Coach:** Last session you said you wanted to look at junctions and in particular when to stop, do you still feel this is a good goal for today?
> **Learner:** Yes, I still feel a bit unsure on them.
> **Coach:** Ok, should we start with a mind map as part of a recap?...

This checking and reconfirming of the goal helps the learner to focus on what is to be covered but also offers the opportunity to change or add to the goal. Perhaps something has happened or occurred to the learner between sessions and they now wish to have this clarified or discussed in the session. Within this dialogue the coach is beginning to move to a recap by use of a mind mapping exercise.

10.1.1 SMART Goals
Frequently the term SMART goal is used. The acronym stands for:

> Specific
> Measureable
> Achievable
> Realistic
> Time bound

We have already covered how to make a Goal specific, achievable and realistic. As for measureable, I see this as being part of a wider process of self-evaluation. With regards to time bound I am not sure this really fits for driver education relating to learner drivers and could be counterproductive. Imagine asking a learner how long they feel it would take them to reach this goal? The answer could be unrealistic or if it was realistic how would they feel if they had not achieved the goal in a preset time period. If the goal is realistic, specific and achievable and the learner is being encouraged to self-evaluate their performance the time element will look after itself.

10.2 R for Reality
In this element of the GROW model the aim is to encourage the learner to identify the reality of the situation. We build our own reality on our beliefs but frequently our beliefs cloud the way we see and interpret the world. The role of the coach is to assist the learner to see the reality for what it really is rather than through rose or dark tinted glasses. This can be extremely challenging both for the coach and for the learner. In the initial sections of this book we discussed how the learner will have their own picture of what is a good driver and it is this picture that will inform their view of driving. The first step in helping to develop this picture is to help the learner recognise the realities of driving and, in so doing, encourage them to challenge their own internal picture.

There are a number of techniques that can help a coach achieve this including:

Description • Third party description

Description and third party description are similar. In description the coach asks the learner to describe the event. In third party description the coach asks the learner to describe the event from the perspective of another person looking in. The key for the coach is to listen carefully and challenge any assumptions the learner has made based on their internal picture of the world.

Coach: Can you describe what happened at that junction for me please?

Learner: Yes – the car pulled out in front of me.

Coach: Why do you feel he did that?

Learner: Because he didn't look.

Coach: How do you know he didn't look?

Learner: Because he pulled out

Coach: Imagine you were him what things may have made it difficult for you to see us?

Learner: There were some parked cars and that group of kids on the corner

Coach: So, how do you know he didn't look?

Learner: I don't, he just might not have been able to see me.

Coach: If you were approaching that situation again is there anything you feel you could have improved?

In this way the coach is encouraging the learner to identify a possible reality that may not have occurred to them. The coach is also helping the learner to consider the reality from different perspectives enabling the learner to better understand the difficulties other drivers face and the need to anticipate these difficulties. With the last question the coach has encouraged the learner to reflect on the situation and identify what learning it offered.

10.3 O for Options

This stage of the model is, in many ways, the key to the coaching model. The aim for the coach here is to encourage the learner to consider a number of options that could further develop their performance. The coach should ask the learner to think about a number of possible options and then explore the benefits and disadvantages of each.

I feel the options stage of the GROW model is probably the most important in driver education as it allows the coach to move past initial answers that the learner may put forward without appearing to judge or be dismissive of these answers. For example:

> **Coach:** Can you think of a situation when you may feel pressured to drive more quickly?
> **Learner:** No, not at all
> **Coach:** OK-imagine you have 3 friends in the car and you are late for an appointment?
> **Learner:** No, that would not bother me, I would just ignore it.
> **Coach:** That could work, could you also think of some other options?
> **Learner:** I am not sure what else I could do! I could try and outline some rules?
> **Coach:** What would be the advantages of that?
> **Learner:** Well they would know what to expect and how to behave
> **Coach:** Can you think of any disadvantages?
> **Learner:** Yes – my mates might just ignore them.
> **Coach:** Ok – Can you think of another option?
> **Learner:** No – not really
> **Coach:** Ok- can I suggest one for you to consider?
> **Learner:** Yes
> **Coach:** Could you say that you felt unwell and want to drive slowly?
> **Learner:** Yes, I could.
> **Coach:** What would be the advantages of that?

Learner: Well they could be OK with that?
Coach: Can you think of any disadvantages?
Learner: Yes – I would have to be a good liar.

The initial option suggested by the learner is one frequently presented but one that may be very difficult to do. Frequently a learner will know this but will offer this type of answer as they believe it will 'tick the box'. In this instance the coach simply moved past this without judging the answer with a simple, yet highly effective, options question.

The coach now has the learner actively reflecting on the real difficulty of coping with this type of situation. The learner then presented a second option. This coach then encouraged the learner to consider the benefits and disadvantages of that option. This is very important as it allows the learner to consider the likelihood of success. Finally when the learner's options were exhausted the coach carefully offered an alternative option for consideration. This was done tactfully with the learner then being offered the opportunity to consider the merits of the suggestion.

10.4 W for Way Forward/What Will You Do?
In this stage of the GROW model the learner is asked to select an option they feel would work for them. In the example used earlier in the options stage, related to peer pressure, the coach would ask the learner to select the option they would use in a similar situation. Once the learner has selected the option then the coach would enquire why they felt that the selected option would work and how they would know if it was successful. This is an important part of the process particularly where the situation being discussed cannot easily be duplicated in a lesson.

If the issue being coached allows you to do so then the selected option should be tested. This is usually quite easy where the issue being considered is related to the simple mechanics of vehicle handling. For example, if practising a reverse manoeuvre simply repeat the exercise.

11. Micro coaching

This is a term I use to describe a coaching session which is narrowly focused on a very specific event that has occurred. Look at the simple diagram below:

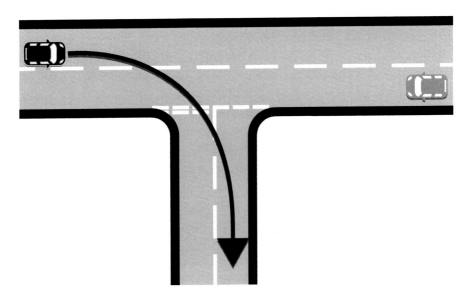

Let's imagine the coach has asked the learner to stop to discuss the situation. Remember in coaching the aim is not to simply improve performance but to develop the learner's ability to self-evaluate their own performance. Below is the type of discussion that may take place.

(Goal question) Coach: Is there anything you feel you could improve on the last junction you completed?

Learner: Yes, I noticed I turned too early.

(Reality question) Coach: Why do you feel that could be an issue?

Learner: Because I could have hit something coming to the end of the road.

(Options question) Coach: How do you feel you could improve next time?

Learner: I could go further forward before I turned.

(Options question) Coach: What do you feel are the benefits of going further forward?
Learner: I would be on the right side of the road as I turned in.
(Options question) Coach: Can you think of any disadvantages?
Learner: Not really.
(Options question) Coach: Could you think of any other ways in which you could have improved the turn?
Learner: I could have tried not to rush across in front of the car.
(Options question) Coach: What would have been the benefits of not rushing in front of the car?
Learner: I would have had more time to look and steer.
(Options question) Coach: Can you think of any disadvantages?
Learner: Not really as there was a gap behind the car.
(Way forward) Coach: Based on what you have said, what would you do next time in that type of situation?
Learner: I would not rush and I would look at the junction.
Coach: Would you like to practise a few more right turns?
Learner: OK.
(Self-monitoring) Coach: Great – this time I will ask you to assess your own turns using a 1 to 10 scale– is that OK?
Learner: Yes – that's fine.

As can be seen in this discussion the coach has used the steps outlined in the GROW model. By use of this approach not only has the coach helped the learner to address the issue of cutting the corner but the learner has also practised how to self-evaluate their performance. In this way the coach has in fact worked on two different levels.

The first level is improving the performance of the learner, the second being the development of the learner's own self evaluation skills. **This is one of the key advantages that coaching offers over instruction, it works on these two levels of performance and self-evaluation.**

I live in the real world and know it is very easy to imagine that the dialogue would not have worked in the way I have outlined. So let's look at the same example but where things have developed slightly differently.

> **(Goal question) Coach:** Is there anything you would like to improve on the last junction?
> **Learner:** Yes, I noticed I turned too early
> **(Reality question) Coach:** Why do you feel that could be an issue?
> **Learner:** Because I could have hit something coming to the end of the road
> **(Options question) Coach:** How do you feel you could improve it next time?
> **Learner:** I could go further forward before I turned
> **(Options question) Coach:** What do you feel are the benefits of going further forward?
> **Learner:** I would be on the right side of the road as I turned in
> **(Options question) Coach:** Can you think of any disadvantages?
> **Learner:** Yes, I would have to slow down a bit more
> **(Options question) Coach:** Why do you feel that would be a disadvantage?
> **Learner:** It would hold the traffic up and slow me down

Here the options questions have really done their work. In this example the options questions are beginning to raise a number of interesting replies that may be showing how the learner is really thinking. The learner's answers are starting to indicate that the real reason for cutting the corner was not lack of knowledge or control but an unwillingness to slow down. This is much more serious and could have been easily missed if the coach had simply accepted the answers presented without exploring the options.

Going forward the coach would now need to consider this and look to develop this theme in the future. This work could start now by asking the learner:

Coach: Why do you feel concerned about holding up the traffic?
Learner: Someone might run into me.
Coach: How could you avoid that do you think?
Learner: Oh... I am not sure to be honest!

At this point the learner has realised the limit of their knowledge and the coach may need to offer a solution, possibly through a set of leading questions.

Coach: When do you feel you may be hit from behind is most likely?
Learner: If I stop suddenly.
Coach: Based on what you have said how could you improve the junction next time?
Learner: I could approach a bit slower.

Whilst I doubt this one piece of discussion will solve the underlying issue the coach has gained a valuable insight, allowing the subject of speed to be revisited later and discussed in more depth. Remember that a driver when being trained will frequently hide their true feelings, thoughts and beliefs and it is these that cause them to reject a great deal of the behaviours advocated in training. Previous 'knowledge' and or 'experience' can be a massive barrier to learning. Of course it can also be a massive help.

To ensure this approach is successful the coach must ask open questions. In the first example the coach used a question which was very open:

(Goal question) Coach: Is there anything you would like to improve on the last junction you completed?

This allowed the learner every opportunity to consider all aspects of the manoeuvre, maximising the self-identification aspect of the exercise. If the learner was unable to identify an area to improve then this would tell the coach that the learner was not aware of any area of improvement and that either their knowledge relating to the manoeuvre or their self-monitoring skills need developing. Once again the initial question has been of great value to the coach.

If a learner is not able to identify an area of improvement the next question the coach should ask should be one that narrows the learner's thought processes.

> **Coach:** Is there anything you would like to improve in relation to your road positioning?
> **Learner:** Well, I think I turned a bit too soon.

Once this is established the coach can now return to the model and work through a set of reality, options and way forward questions.

The diagram below provides a simple outline of the approach outlined in this section. The black path shows the route the coach would take if the learner was able to self-identify an area of improvement. The white path shows the approach required where the learner cannot self identify an area of improvement.

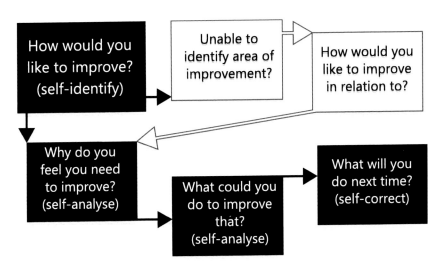

11.1 Scaling

Another common tool used by coaches is scaling. **Scaling** aims to help the learner to assess themselves and, most importantly, to identify areas of further improvement. The technique is a deceptively simple one.

The first step is to ask the learner to scale themselves using a 1 to 10 scale, with one being poor and 10 being very good, on how well they think they had just done with regards to x. In most cases the learner will give themselves a score below 10. The next step is to ask the learner why they have given that score. This is then followed up with an options question by the coach: 'What are your options to improve your score?'

Once again the focus of the coach is to aid the learner to evaluate their own performance and look to develop solutions to any problems identified.

Scaling works very well with the general structure of the GROW model being followed. This example looks at how you could use scaling for a reverse park exercise.

> **Coach**: On a scale of 1 to 10 with 1 being poor and 10 being very good, how would you rate yourself the reverse park you have just completed?
>
> **Learner:** I would give myself a 7.
>
> **Coach:** Why do you feel a 7?
>
> **Learner:** Well, I felt I was just looking out the back and not really for other traffic.
>
> **Coach:** How could you improve that, do you feel?
>
> **Learner:** I could look around more.
>
> **Coach:** Is there anything you can think of that would help you look around more?
>
> **Learner:** I could go slower.
>
> **Coach:** How could you do that?
>
> **Learner:** Using clutch control.
>
> **Coach:** So what will you do next time?
>
> **Learner**: Control my speed and look around more.

Of course this is a really simplified version of the discussion but does demonstrate the basic principles.

The main criticism of this approach is that the learner's own score may not truly reflect the reality.

> **Coach:** On a scale of 1 to 10 with 1 being poor and 10 being very good, how would you rate yourself the reverse park you have just completed?
> **Learner:** It was great! A 10!

If this does occur it tells the coach a great deal about the learners understanding of what is required and their ability to analyse themselves, and this in itself is a worthwhile discovery.

As with the micro coaching the next step would be to narrow the focus:

> **Coach:** On a scale of 1 to 10 with 1 being poor and 10 being very good, how would you rate yourself the reverse park you have just completed?
> **Learner:** It was great! A 10!
> **Coach:** On a scale of 1 to 10 how would you rate your observation?
> **Learner:** Well, I only looked around once so not so great, about a 6.
> **Coach:** So, how do you think that would reflect in your initial scale?
> **Learner:** Oh probably on an 8 now I think about it.

In the initial question the coach offered the opportunity to consider all aspects of the exercise. When the answer was poor the coach narrowed the question and pointed the learner to the issue. Over a period of time the learner will develop their ability to narrow their own thought processes in this way, which is an important step in the development of their own self-evaluation scales.

Some learners will lack confidence and score themselves low, particularly if they are anxious. This is not really a problem as when they repeat the exercise and improve they will adjust their scores accordingly.

Another use of scaling is to raise awareness by using a scale to self-monitor performance. This is a great technique, for example when trying to improve observation. The coach asks the learner on a scale of 1 to 10 how far ahead they are looking. The learner may give a 7, the coach then asks them to self-monitor as they continue to drive. The coach should ask the learner occasionally during the drive what score they would give themselves now for observation. Over a period the learner may naturally improve as their self-monitoring and self-awareness builds.

There are a couple of issues a coach needs be aware of when using the scaling technique. The first is to make the scale specific. Asking a learner to scale a full session is not going to tell the coach or the learner a great deal. What are they scaling, if they have enjoyed the session, if they improved, if they were anxious? To be successful the scale needs to be specific.

The other issue is failing to use the scale as a means to assist the learner to develop. A common failing I have seen is where the coach has asked for a scale but did not follow up with a question along the lines of 'how would you improve the score?' The aim of the scale is to raise awareness and to assist the learner to develop ideas about how to improve, so the coach must include the question of 'how would you improve the score?' The exception to this is where a scale is being used to build self-awareness, such as in the observation exercise discussed earlier.

The final issue is the coach jumping in when the scale score does not fit with their assessment. This often occurs when the learner has given themselves a score the coach feels is too low:

Coach: Don't be so hard on yourself, it was better than a 2

©eDriving Solutions Ltd

This removes the self-evaluation concept. In these instances the best thing to do is to encourage the learner to explain their reasoning for the score.

A final word on scaling. The feedback I have received on this technique has been extremely positive and based on this feedback I have discovered a new and exciting phenomenon which I have called 'random numbers'. This manifests itself when a learner turns a corner or carries out a manoeuvre and then for no reason says a number like 'Seven'. A shocked instructor then replies saying 'seven?' The learner then says, 'yes I was a bit wide, I should have slowed down.' You know you are on to a winner when this happens to you....your learners are self-evaluating!

12. Structuring a Session
This section looks at how you could structure a session and gives an example. It also revisits one of the most exciting elements of coaching for me, using coaching to help the learner to consider how they will respond to 'real life driving'. This section draws heavily on the structure developed as part of the EU-funded HERMES project. Appendix A to this book provides you with an example relating to a turn in the road and a blank copy so you can develop your own session plans. Always remember that the plan needs to be highly flexible to allow the learner to lead the session. This flexibility is at the heart of learner centred approaches.

12.1 In the Driver's Seat
In this stage the coach needs to consider a number of issues. The first is to settle the learner down and look for any signs that would indicate the learner's state of mind. Here simple questions such as: How are you? Have you had a good few days? etc. will allow the coach to assess the learner's emotional state. It is worth just highlighting that the coach will be as interested in the non-verbal communication (e.g. level of eye contact, body posture, facial expression, etc.) as what is said.

Within this stage the coach will need to consider contracting. **Contracting** is a process by which the coach discusses how the session will operate. The idea is to discuss what coaching is, how it works and how it will benefit the learner. Frequently this will overlap into goals but it may also be necessary to consider it here, particularly if a new approach is to be taken or if the learner is new or relatively new to the coach. You should carefully consider going through a contracting phase with all your learners after reading this book as they may be surprised by many of the techniques you may now wish to introduce and you need to assist them to understand how these techniques will benefit them.

Finally, within this stage, the coach also needs to be considering how they can maximise the learner's feeling of being **responsible for the safety of the vehicle** without raising the learner's level of anxiety. When delivering coaching workshops I frequently ask the instructors attending if they ask their pupils who is responsible for the safety of the vehicle. In many cases the instructors indicate that when they do ask, the pupil often says the instructor. This is worrying as it would indicate that for many drivers the first time they drive a vehicle and really feel responsible for it is possibly when they are on test or on their first drive after passing. Therefore part of this stage of the coaching session is to maximise the learner's feeling of responsibility whilst not overloading them. In instruction quite often the transfer of responsibility is not stated. The instructor simply stops talking and reduces the input and this quite often leaves the learner unsure of who really is responsible for safety. This needs to be made clear so the learner is fully aware of their responsibilities, if not at the start of a lesson then at an appropriate time in the lesson. This may start with taking charge of a set exercise, for example by asking a question like: How would you like to take full responsibility for the next turn in the road? But eventually this needs to build up so the learner understands that when they are in the driving seat they are responsible.

Please do not take this to mean that the coach would not step in or that this advice overrides legal issues. It does not, this is a question of getting the driver, as much as possible, to recognise that they are morally responsible for their actions because the moment they take to the road without a supervising driver they are both morally and legally responsible.

12.2 Goal Setting

The next stage is to set or review the coaching goals for the session. Goal setting has already been covered in section 10.1 so all I will do is remind you that the goal should ideally have been discussed on the previous session and should now be reviewed and reconfirmed to ensure that the learner has not had a change of mind and wishes to cover an alternative goal. If it was not possible on a previous session then a discussion of the goals for the session should be done, remembering to fully maximise the inclusion of the learner in this process.

12.3 Problem Solving

The next stage is to encourage the learner to consider the problem. As discussed in section 7 this problem solving approach may take the form of a mind mapping exercise or simply a set of open questions. Case studies can also be used or you can give the learner a scenario to consider. The key element here is to ensure the learner has a clear view of the problem they need to solve before moving to the solution.

12.4 Task Repetition and Self-evaluation

In this stage of the model session the focus is on developing the performance of the learner for the particular exercise being completed. Of course, as with all elements of coaching, the focus should be on the development of the learner's own ability to self-evaluate their performance. Micro coaching is likely to be used extensively in this element of the model. See section 11.

12.5 Changing Context

Whilst you may not include this stage in every session, it is without doubt vital. **I would even go as far as to say that if you do not cover this section all you are doing in reality is preparing someone to pass a driving test!**

In our instructor workshops we ask 'what is the purpose of the journey on a driving lesson?' The groups quickly say 'to learn.' However, once the learner has passed the driving test few, if any, journeys they may make will take place in a context where the goal is **purely** to learn. Nearly all journeys we make have other goals such as arriving on time, in the right place, dealing with passengers, etc. As we have already discussed in section 2 context has a major influence on behaviour. **Have you ever done anything you would not normally say or do because of where you are, who you are with or what you are trying to achieve?** Put simply, we frequently behave differently in different contexts. It is therefore vital that a coach encourages the learner to consider different scenarios and how different contexts could influence driving related decisions. To do this the coach needs to encourage the learner to consider a situation that moves the learner's thought processes from the current context to future journeys.

There are many ways to do this. For example when asking the learner to make a turn in the road, ask them to do it quickly as you are really pushed for time. In this case not only have you added some time pressures but also some pressure from an important other – you. It is amazing how these two pressures will influence the learner's performance. Once the manoeuvre is complete the coach would need to carefully discuss how the performance had been affected and ask why the learner had been able or unable to resist the pressure. It is vital that the learner is encouraged to consider the issues and project themselves forward to times when they could be affected by these pressures. For example when out driving with friends and they ask the driver to hurry up.

Once the issues have been explored the coach should encourage the learner to develop **coping strategies** that would enable the learner to deal with the issues. When designing and facilitating a scenario to explore changing contexts the coach needs to consider three questions:

> What is the issue being explored?
> How does it influence the individual driver?
> What are the coping strategies?

Below are some simple examples of scenarios you may wish to use.

Motorway (Fatigue)

> **Coach:** What do you feel are the issues you would face driving home late at night on a motorway?

Rural roads (Peer pressure)

> **Coach:** Imagine you were driving home with 3 friends after a night out, can you think of any way in which that situation may affect your driving?

In-town driving (Time pressures)

> **Coach:** How do you feel being late for an important appointment might influence your driving?

There are also 60 more detailed scenarios provided in the HERMES project and these can be downloaded for free on the link below:

http://www.alles-fuehrerschein.at/HERMES/index.php?page=objective

12.6 Self-evaluation of the session

In this final stage the learner should be encouraged to review the session and identify further areas of development. This should be linked to the goals for the next session. A word of caution here, it is very easy to just simply look at performance and to forget that coaching is also about feelings. The coach should remember that if the learner is not confident in their ability then this will raise anxiety, therefore even if the learner appears to be competent the coach should allow them to re-visit any areas that they feel need to be developed further.

13. Challenging the Beliefs

Up until now we have looked at coaching as a means of developing performance. In this section we will discuss another model of coaching called Cognitive Behavioural Coaching (CBC). CBC is based on Cognitive Behavioural Therapy (CBT) and the starting point for CBT is that our beliefs influence the way we interpret the world. However, quite often our beliefs are twisted or too generalised. For example, if we believe all drivers are just getting in our way we will become frustrated and annoyed and we may become aggressive. On the other hand if we believe that generally drivers do their best we are more likely to be tolerant and understanding.

Probably the model most widely used in CBC is ABCDE this stands for:
Activating situation
Belief
Consequential emotions
Disputing the belief
Exchanging the thought

and there are many ways in which CBC could be used in driving education. An excellent example is where a learner is very anxious or is a perfectionist and who early on in learning something new over-reacts to a mistake that most learners would make during the initial learning process.

So let's imagine that this perfectionist hits the kerb whilst practising a left hand reverse. This would be the **Activating** event. The **Belief** would be, I am a perfectionist and cannot make mistakes, and this belief could possibly raise the **Consequential** emotions of frustration, anger and anxiety.

To deal with this the coach must encourage the learner to consider if their belief is correct or if it is a generalisation. This phase is called **Disputing** the belief.

The coach should also encourage the learner to consider if the belief and resulting behaviour had helped or hindered the outcome. This question sequence may follow this outline:

> **Coach:** What did you feel in that situation?
>
> **Learner:** I was really annoyed with myself for getting it wrong.
>
> **Coach:** Why did you become annoyed?
>
> **Learner:** Because I know I can do it, I hate getting things wrong.
>
> **Coach:** How do you think getting annoyed affects your ability to learn?
>
> **Learner:** Well, it's not good as I get frustrated.
>
> **Coach:** What feelings help you learn best?
>
> **Learner:** Well I suppose not getting annoyed and keeping cool
>
> **Coach:** What can you do to keep cool?
>
> **Learner:** I am not sure.
>
> **Coach:** If you were giving some advice to someone about staying cool what advice would you give?
>
> **Learner:** I would probably say no one is perfect and it is part of learning.
>
> **Coach:** How would you feel about that in this instance?
>
> **Learner:** It is good advice I suppose – I could give it a try.

In this way the coach is **Disputing** the driver's preconceived ideas and encouraging them to **Exchange** them for more helpful thoughts and beliefs.

I am sure as you have read this section you will be thinking to yourself that these questions are quite prying and deep. They are, and to work you will need to develop an excellent level of rapport with the learner. Before starting this sequence it would be beneficial, and will reduce resistance, to ask the learner if they would mind if you asked them about how their feelings influence their driving and learning.

14. Your Own Performance

I hope now you are nearing the end of the book you are becoming excited about trying many of the tools and approaches discussed. However, how will you feel when first implementing these ideas and techniques?

When you change something as fundamental as your approaches to learning it will undoubtedly feel strange and difficult. This is normal and to be expected with change. In fact there is an argument that would say, if you don't get these feeling of awkwardness and unfamiliarity you probably have not changed very much. You therefore need to expect these feelings and work through them. At the other end you will find that you will gain more satisfaction from your role as an instructor and your learners will have greatly benefited.

Try and make this initial period easy on yourself, introduce these concepts slowly, initially start with learners who are responsive before introducing these concepts to more challenging learners; you need to build up your own experience and confidence first. As the saying goes, Rome was not built in a day!

You should also give some thought as to how your learners will respond. Switching from instructor led to learner centred approaches will be a shock to your learners, and you will need to consider this carefully. For this reason contracting is very important (section 12) as this helps the learner to understand how these approaches work and the benefits they will bring.

14.1 Developing Your Skills

I am sure that as you have read this book you will have noted that you could easily apply the self-evaluation techniques to your own driving and to your own tuition skills.

A good way of self-evaluating your own coaching performance is to use a **self-reflective log**. These can be very useful as they help you to think about your performance and assist you to develop your own self-evaluation techniques. After you have delivered a session put aside 15 minutes to jot down how you felt the session went. What you could improve and further develop. How you felt and how this influenced the learner.

On the next page is a simple template that may help you. An A4 copy of this template is available at http://www.edrivingsolutions.com/book.aspx

Questions	Your answers
How good was the rapport on the lesson?	
How could I improve my non-verbal communication skills?	
How relaxed did the learner appear?	
How could these aspects be improved?	
How did I feel?	
How focused was I on the lesson?	
What went well on the lesson? What could I do to further develop this or maximise this on all my lessons?	
What element(s) of the lesson could I further improve? How could this be achieved?	
How open were my questions? How could I effectively use more open questions?	
Who did most of the talking? How could I encourage the learner to engage and be more active in the lesson?	

Once you have done this a number of times you will probably see a pattern emerging. Once you have this then start to consider how you can develop your own GROW plan to help further develop your skills.

Below is a simple set of questions that may help you to develop your own GROW plan:

Your GROW plan	Your answers
What element of your coaching would you like to further improve?	
This is where a **SMART** goal would be useful: **Specific** – what will you do **Measureable** – what will success look like **Achievable** – how will you do it **Realistic** – is what you are proposing realistic **Time measures** – how long will it take	
Why do you feel this area needs further development?	
What are your options to improve? Try and identify 3 possible options and list the advantages and disadvantages for each?	
Option 1	
Option 2	
Option 3	
From the options above what will you do over the next 3 months? Try and be as precise as you can.	

Once you have completed your GROW plan you will need to consider how you will monitor it. I set review dates in my calendar but how you do it is up to you – it is your GROW plan.

Copies of both these forms can be downloaded at http://www.edrivingsolutions.com/book.aspx

So what is stopping you?

14.2 Using Video

A useful tool to evaluate your own performance is the use of video. There are a couple of ethical and data protection issues to consider here - so be careful. The first is that you need the informed consent of the learner. What I mean here is that the learner must fully understand what the video is to be used for, how it will be kept safe and handled and to whom it may be shown. You cannot ask to film a video to help you review your performance and then decide to place it on YouTube! - unless you have permission from the learner to do so. I would always recommend that you develop a form that clearly defines how the video will be used and have the learner sign it. You should also consider how the video will be destroyed when the time comes.

When setting the camera, try and place it so you can see both yourself and the learner. When reviewing pay particular attention to:

> Your and their tone of voice
> Non-verbal communication between you and the learner
> Levels of eye contact
> How you encouraged engagement using active listening techniques
> Who was doing most of the talking
> If your questions were truly open or if they were leading or judgemental
> How you used problem solving exercises
> How you used coaching models

When you watch the video, closely analyse your performance as video is great for observing non-verbal communication. It also offers you the opportunity to hear what you have said so make sure you listen, try and place yourself in the position of the learner and ask yourself how did the learner interpret what you had said?

14.3 Using Coaching on Check Tests

There should be no problem using coaching techniques on a Continued Ability and Fitness to Give Instructor (Check test). The feedback we have received from instructors who have completed coaching workshops with us is that grades have gone up or have stayed the same. Where the grades have stayed the same the instructors had already been previously awarded a grade 6. We have had this feedback with both role play and with real pupils. What is particularly pleasing, and shows the Driving Standards Agency are supporting coaching and learner centred approaches, is that the examiners have generally commented that a learner centred approach had been used to good effect. If you are in any doubt about using coaching on a check test then please contact ourselves or the Driving Standards Agency who will be able to advise you on this issue.

See Appendix B to this book where you will find an excellent article written by Dave Parkin of eDriving Solutions about his recent Fleet check test. Of course you need to bear in mind there is effective and ineffective coaching and just like Dave you will need to show effective coaching on your check test.

15. Final Word
Coaching and learner centred approaches offer many benefits over simple fault based correction and instruction. When we simply tell a learner how to do something we may be missing an opportunity for the learner to practice one of the most critical skills they need to develop as a driver – their own ability to self-evaluate. This is what coaching and learner centred approaches offer, they focus on the development of this most critical skill and, in so doing, raise the learner's own level of awareness and responsibility.

When I started this book my goal was to provide a text that an instructor could use to develop their skills. I hope I have done that for you and that you will find this book, and subsequent books I intend to write, a useful reference. My view of learner centred and coaching approaches to driver education are different to anyone else's I have met and the view in this book is very much my own, based on my own experience. I hope you have enjoyed this view and that you feel you have benefitted from it.

Coaching itself is changing and developing quickly and for that reason it has simply not been possible to provide a complete view of coaching in this book. There are so many different approaches and techniques, and below are a couple of general coaching books you may consider reading if you wish to explore the subject further.

Coaching for Performance:
Sir John Whitmore

Excellence in Coaching:
Jonathan Passmore

Cognitive Behavioural Coaching Techniques for Dummies:
Helen Whitten

You may also find a great deal of information from the bibliography at the back of this book.

If you would like to attend one of our workshops then visit http://www.edrivingsolutions.com/cpdcourses.aspx to see if we are running an event near you. Or contact us directly on www.edrivingsolutions.com

As I say at all my workshops, I would be delighted to hear from you. Feedback is gratefully received, both good and bad. If you have any questions, or you wish to give feedback on this book and the approaches advocated then please do not hesitate to contact me: http://www.edrivingsolutions.com/ContactUs.aspx

Appendices

Appendix A

A Semi-Structured Coaching Plan.

I have provided 2 copies of this form, one is a blank copy (below), which you can also download as A4 pdf version at http://www.edrivingsolutions.com/book.aspx, and one gives a simple example using a turn in the road.

Based on HERMES 2010   Blank form:

HERMES Model	Aims to be achieved
Making it clear they are in the driving seat	
Identify the goals	
Mind map the task	
Encourage self-reflection on performance	
Task repetition	
Identify obstacles (Change the context)	
Commit to the strategy	
Develop self-assessment	

Example: Turn in the Road

HERMES Model	Possible questions asked by the instructor	Aims to be achieved
Making it clear they are in the driving seat	How are you today? How do you feel about driving today? Who do you think should be responsible for our and other people's safety today? As the driver is there anything that you feel could affect our safety today?	Encouraging the pupil to identify that they are/ should be responsible for safety as the driver.
Identify the goals	Last session we discussed that our next step forward is to look at a Turn in the Road, how would you feel about doing that today? How did you get on with the self-study tasks you set yourself last session? What do you feel are the main things to consider for completing a turn in the road?	To identify the goals for the session with -in a wider curriculum To ensure that the previously agreed goals are still appropriate To gain feedback on the self study that was agreed on the previous session. To encourage the pupil to identify their personal goals for the session and a success criteria
Mind map the task	What dangers do you feel you need to consider with this exercise? Before we start the turn in the road could you outline for me what you are trying to achieve? (Instructor should record this as a mind mapping exercise) Do you feel the approach you have outlined minimises the risks you identified? Is there anything else you could do to reduce the risks?	For the pupil to identify the risks associated with the exercise and to develop a personal picture of how to reduce these risks. Note: The mind map should be revisited and amended or added to as the pupil self-discovers new things.

HERMES Model	Possible questions asked by the instructor	Aims to be achieved
Encourage self-reflection on performance	How would you feel about attempting a turn in the road here? How did you feel you did? What elements would you like to improve? How could you improve that? How would you assess the turn in the road you have just completed using a 1 to 10 scale? What could you do to improve your score? Is there anything you found out that you would like to add to your mind map?	To develop the skills required to complete a turn in the road safely.
Task repetition	The previous step should be repeated with the instructor encouraging the learner to focus on more specific elements as they improve. eg control, observation, etc. Can I ask you to consider this please?	Development of skills base through the development of the pupils own self assessment skills
Identify obstacles (Change the context)	Context scenario You are late for a very important appointment and take a wrong turning and have to do a turn in the road. What do you think you could feel in that situation? How do you think these feelings could affect your judgement?	Change context and encourage consideration of how 'human factors' impact on performance Consider positives and negatives for a number of proposed options Note: over a number of sessions the pupil could be introduced to a number of other scenarios

HERMES Model	Possible questions asked by the instructor	Aims to be achieved
Identify obstacles (Change the context) CONT.	Do you think that could impact on the safety of what you are doing? How could you reduce this impact (possible coping strategy)? What would prevent you from doing that (refers to pupil's possible coping strategy) do you think? Are there any other options do you think? (Alternative coping strategy(s)) Can you see any issues that would prevent you from doing that (refers to pupil's alternative coping strategy(s) do you think?	Change context and encourage consideration of how 'human factors' impact on performance Consider positives and negatives for a number of proposed options Note: over a number of sessions the pupil could be introduced to a number of other scenarios
Commit to the strategy	So what will you do in that situation (situation outlined above)?	Commit to a coping strategy
Develop self-assessment	Overall how do you feel you have done today? (Possible 1 to 10 scaling) What could you do to further develop? How could you do that over the ... (could be linked to self study)? How would you summarise this session? What would be your goals for next the session? Do you feel there is anything you could do to help you achieve that goal between now and the next session?	Self-assess performance Maximise the pupil's responsibility for their own self-development Development of a self summary Set goals for next sessions Note: If possible pupil should be given a copy of their personal mind map

Appendix B: My Fleet Check Test

By Dave Parkin (eDriving Solutions)

This article is a brief description of my recent check test. I have tried to make it as factual as possible in the hope that it can help other instructors to consider their approach.

I had chosen to do role play for my Check Test. The examiner gave me the brief of what the check test would consist of. He then gave me the option of giving him directions (me deciding the route) or him giving the directions and me feeding them back (him deciding the route). I chose the latter. I was told that the licence check and eyesight had been done so we made our way to the car (I asked him to read a car number plate at the appropriate distance before he started to drive just for good measure anyway).

Into Role and into the car

I explained what today's session was to consist of and emphasised that it was not a test and that I was there to see how he drove and help him to discover if there was anything in his driving that he could improve upon. I asked him what type of driving he did and the type of vehicle that most of his work related driving was done in. He told me that his main work was taking spares to various customers as and when they required them and that he did about 20,000 work miles a year. He told me that he had been sent by his boss and said "that he had not had a crash or anything".

We then went through a short presentation on road risk (this is now freely available to all members of eDriving Solutions) on the laptop in the car. After about five minutes the examiner came out of role and stopped the presentation and asked me to briefly tell him what the rest of the presentation would cover. I then moved onto car safety checks. I asked what things he should check on the car before driving. He told me that there was someone at his work who was responsible for the servicing etc.

of the company vehicles and that they looked after that side of things. We discussed which parts of the vehicle were important to his safety, which led to a discussion about tyres and who was actually responsible for his safety when driving. This was followed by a breakdown of POWDERS. During this part the examiner slipped in a question about licensing and informing the DVLA about a change of address. I ensured that he was familiar with the vehicle controls.

Into the driving assessment

We moved away safely from the side of the road and accelerated. I questioned his knowledge of the speed limit on the road (20mph) which he said was 30 mph. I informed him that it was 20mph and he levelled off accordingly.

The next fault was incorrect position for a right turn, totally straddling the centre line, commenting on a van that was parked too close to the junction, asking if parking there was allowed (I mentioned 10m but the van was in a marked bay). Mirror checks were made after the signal was given.

Right at a roundabout. The left signal to leave wasn't cancelled until after a junction on the left. Left at the next roundabout. He got very close to the vehicle in front when queuing and commented on its driver not emerging immediately and showing impatience towards its driver. On emerging he accelerated harshly up to the speed limit.

The next three roundabouts we followed the road ahead with all mirror checks being late. Next roundabout right, again with late mirror checks and did not check left side before taking the exit. Finally we took a right turn and pulled up on the left in a safe and convenient place, yet again all mirror checks came after the signal.

Throughout the assessment drive I made a note of any issues that needed discussion, which were; Mirrors after, position right turn, left signal too long, tyres and tarmac, impatience, eco driving, no left check at roundabout. In all the assessment drive only lasted about ten minutes.

Discussing key risks Identified

I opened with "If I were to ask you to give yourself a score out of ten for the short drive that you have just done, what would you give yourself?" He gave himself a nine. So then I asked him to score himself on his use of mirrors. He gave himself a ten! Mmm. I then moved on to the timing of his mirror checks, discussing MSM and why he needed to check before rather than after the event. Next the right turn position, we spoke about the advantages and disadvantages of positioning in this way, leaving the left signal on inappropriately, not leaving adequate clearance when in queuing traffic and checking the left side when exiting roundabouts.

I addressed the impatience issue by asking what his issues with the other driver were. His main concern was regarding not emerging when they could have. Therefore holding everyone up. I asked if there may be any times when he may not emerge when he could. This caused discussion on things like, being lost and being distracted.

Eco Driving was discussed using advantages and disadvantages of harsh acceleration, smooth acceleration, late braking, planning ahead, and using appropriate gear for speed. The remaining time was used to ensure that the risks identified were addressed using coaching methods. By the end of this part the driver had clearly improved the way in which he was dealing with the situations that he faced.

The session was concluded by completing an appraisal form with the driver relating to the initial drive, recapping any issues that were identified, and discussing and agreeing what he would do to improve his driving. This was recorded on the appraisal form and given to the Driver.

Next the short wait while the appropriate paperwork was completed followed by the debrief from the examiner. He was pleased that I had used "a client-centred approach" (coaching) and was very happy with what he had seen awarding me a grade 6.

Appendix C: CRITICAL ELEMENTS OF COACHING - AN AIDE MEMOIR

Aims of Coaching:

Increase awareness and responsibility in the learner

To build rapport and confidence in a relaxed, constructive environment

Make the learner both the learner and teacher

Learner learns to judge their own performance

Learner takes ownership of the learning

The coach must:

Use positive reinforcement to build confidence

Build the rapport between themselves and the learner as one of equals

Be non judgemental

Have a good level of emotional intelligence (EQ) – be aware of

your own emotional state
your learner's
and have the ability to modify your own behaviour

Enable the learner to develop self-evaluation skills

Actively listen

Enable themselves to develop self-reflective skills

The basic toolbox for coaching includes:

Use **open** questions and positive feedback

Active listening:
watching, matching, repeating, construction, reflection

Develop **problem solving** skills in the learner:
use Mind mapping techniques
use scenarios
use case studies

Learning **investment** - place the learner in the active role of producing their own knowledge

Develop **self evaluation** skills – there are 4 continuous stages:
self-monitoring – monitor performance
self-identification - identify learning triggers
self-analysis – identify number of solutions or coping strategies
self-development – implement an appropriate coping strategy

Scaling : 1-10 tool to develop self-assessment skills, identify areas for further improvement

A Coaching Development Model: GROW

G = Goals. Set goals in a structured way (see below), allow learner to feed into the process
Goals should be **SMART:**

Specific
Measurable
Achievable
Realistic
Timely

R = Reality. The learner recognises the realities of driving
O = Options. Learner considers a number of options to develop their performance
W = What will you do? Practise to ensure the option is successful

Structuring a Session:

Contracting – Driver's Responsibility (discuss how the session will operate)
Goal setting (review and re-confirm)
Problem solving (use questions, mindmaps, case studies)
Task Repetition (develop learner's performance & self evaluation skills)
Changing context (consider how different situations could influence driving decisions)
Self evaluation of the session (review session – identify areas for further development)

Evaluating your Own Performance:

Complete a self-reflective log after each session
Develop your own GROW plan to extend your own skills
Monitor your plan and use it

Bibliography

1,6,7,- HERMES (2010). *EU Hermes project Final report - High impact approach for Enhancing Road safety through More Effective communication Skills* In the context of category B driver training. *Retrieved from: http://ec.europa.eu/transport/road_safety/pdf/projects/hermes_final_report_en.pdf on 10 March 2010.*

2 - Engstrom, I., Gregersen, N. P., Hernetkoski, K., Keskinen, E., & Nyberg, A., (2003). *Young and Novice Drivers, Driver Education and Training – Literature Review,* Swedish National Road and Transport Research Institute: Sweden.

3 - Parker, D., and Stradling, S., (2001) *Road Safety Research Report No 17 Influencing Driver Attitudes and Behaviour.,* West Yorkshire; Department of Environment, Transport and the Regions.

4 - Keskinen, E., Peräaho, M., and Laapotti, S., (2010) Goals For Driver Education (GDE) 5 –SOC matrix., Presented at The Joint 3rd Scientific NORBIT Conference and 5th Japanese-Nordic Conference on Traffic and Transportation Psychology. Turku,. Finland.

5 - Boud, A., (1995). (Ed by; Boud, D.) *Enhancing learning through self-assessment.,* Routledge Falmer., West Sussex: UK.

8 - Edwards I (2010) A model of Self-evaluation: NORBIT Conference Turku Finland, Unpublished work

9 - Whitmore, J. (2002). *Coaching for performance.* London, UK: Nicholas Brealey.